Miss Rhew

MOUNTAINS

Troll Associates

MOUNTAINS

by Keith Brandt

Illustrated by Art Cumings

Troll Associates

Library of Congress Cataloging in Publication Data

Brandt, Keith, (date)
  Mountains.

  Summary: Text and illustrations describe how
mountains are formed, their varying characteristics, and
how they are being continually changed by the forces of
nature.
  1. Mountains—Juvenile literature. [1. Mountains]
I. Cumings, Art, ill. II. Title.
GB512.B73   1984   551.4 '32   84-2577
ISBN 0-8167-0154-7 (lib. bdg.)
ISBN 0-8167-0155-5 (pbk.)

A mountain range is a magnificent sight. Looking like the bony spine of a huge animal, it stretches across the horizon as far as the eye can see. It sends jagged peaks disappearing into clouds far above the Earth's surface. The mountains look as if they have been there forever. But they haven't.

Scientists believe that, when the Earth was formed many millions of years ago, there were no mountains or valleys, no deserts, and no oceans. At first, the surface of the planet was very hot. Then the Earth began to cool, and its outer crust hardened into rock. Later, oceans and continents formed, and mountains started to appear.

There are four main kinds of mountains— volcanic mountains, dome mountains, folded mountains, and fault block mountains.

Volcanic mountains were created by violent volcanic activity deep inside the Earth. Under its crust, our planet is a furnace of incredibly hot liquid rock called magma.

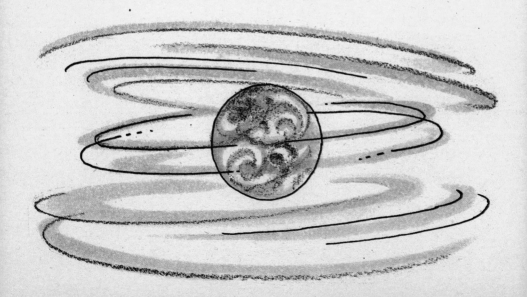

Sometimes pressure inside the Earth builds up. It forces the magma to the surface, where it erupts into the air as a volcano. The molten rock, known as lava, cools and hardens after it pours out of the volcano. Each time a volcano erupts, more lava flows from its crater. The lava piles up and up, forming a larger and higher volcanic mountain.

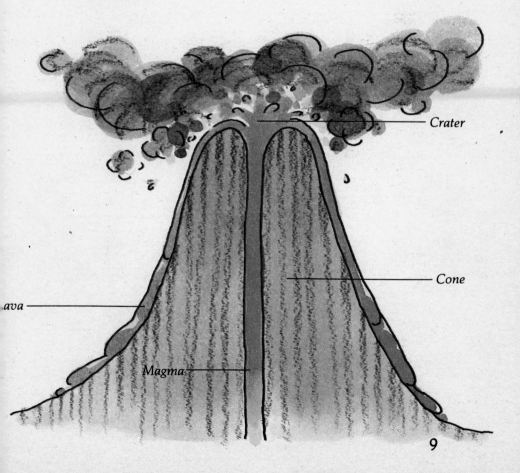

Crater

Cone

Lava

Magma

Other mountains were formed in other ways. Dome mountains were formed when underground forces caused the Earth's crust to be pushed up into smooth dome shapes. The Black Hills of South Dakota are dome mountains.

Folded mountains were formed when the Earth's crust wrinkled and folded because of horizontal pressures. The Appalachian Mountains are folded mountains.

And fault block mountains were formed when movements below the surface broke the Earth's crust into blocks and forced the broken pieces upward. The Sierra Nevada mountains in California are fault block mountains.

Mountain-building has never been limited to dry land. Mountains have also formed along the ocean floors. The Hawaiian Islands are really the tops of volcanic mountains. They are so tall that they rise high above the surface of the water.

Some of the most spectacular mountain ranges in the world have never been seen because they are submerged in thousands of feet of water. One of these mountain ranges is called the Mid-Atlantic Ridge. It runs north and south through the middle of the Atlantic Ocean. It was first discovered only a little more than 100 years ago, during the laying of the first telegraph cables from Europe to America.

New mountains are growing all the time, because the forces that form them never stop. But other forces of nature are also constantly at work, wearing down the world's mountains. This wearing-down process is called erosion.

Wind erodes mountains, tearing off tiny bits of rock and carrying them away and dropping them somewhere else. Rain and

melting snow also erode mountains. As the waters run down the mountainside, they cut grooves into the rock. Soil is washed away and carried into the valley below.

As the years go by, the grooves get deeper and wider. The Grand Canyon, of Arizona, is more than a mile deep. This awesome groove was cut by the waters of the Colorado River as it ran over the rocks.

Sometimes seeds take root between the rocks on a mountain and begin to grow. The plants and trees they become then push soil and stones off the mountainside. Some even split big boulders as they grow. In this way, plants also help to erode mountains.

Glaciers also slowly erode mountains. A glacier is a huge mass of ice and snow that slowly moves down a slope. As glaciers move, they scrape and rub and press against the rocks under them. They break off chunks of rock and carry them along.

Millions of years ago, during the ice ages, glaciers covered much of North America. As the weather warmed and the ice-age glaciers melted, they left deposits of rocks that had been scraped from the mountainsides. The rocky soil that covers parts of the northeast United States was laid down by moving glaciers long ago.

As the forces of nature change mountains, mountains also act on nature. When winds carrying moisture-filled clouds reach mountain ranges, they are stopped by the high peaks. This causes the winds and clouds to rise into the cold upper air. There, the moisture condenses into rain or snow. It falls on the windward side of the mountains.

In the Northern Hemisphere of the world, the winds usually blow from west to east. That is why the mountains along the west coast of North America are rich and green on their west side and dry on their east side. The moisture that the winds pick up as they flow over the Pacific Ocean is dropped on the windward side of the mountain barrier. As a result, some of the driest deserts in North America lie just east of this mountain barrier.

Even in warm climates there may be snow at the tops of the tallest mountains all year. The reason is that at high altitudes, the air is thin and dry and cold. It holds less of the sun's warmth, so the snow never melts.

If you stood at the base of a very high mountain on a summer day, you would be comfortable in thin clothing. If you climbed halfway up the mountain, you would need to wear a sweater or a light jacket to be comfortable. But at the top of the mountain, you would need to wear a winter jacket and gloves!

Mountain climbers always carry warm clothing. They know that, for every thousand feet they climb, the air temperature drops three degrees Fahrenheit.

In a way, climbing a mountain is like traveling from a warm country to a cold country.

Because the temperature is different at various heights on a mountain, its plant life is different, too. At the foot of a mountain, you will probably find good soil and rich vegetation. Trees will grow tall here, and many kinds of plants will flourish.

As you climb the mountain, you will see fewer kinds of plants. You won't see many broad-leafed trees, such as oak and maple and aspen. Instead, you will see more and more hardy evergreen trees. Also, the trees part-way up a mountain don't grow as tall as they do in the valley. That's because the cold temperature creates a shorter growing season. There may also be less moisture on the slope for plant roots to use.

As you climb higher, you will reach an area known as an alpine meadow. Here, there are just a few stunted trees clinging to the mountainside, weedy grasses, and only the hardiest flowers and plants. These, too, fade from view as you continue to climb.

Now the only kinds of plant life around are lichens and mosses. They grow in cracks on windswept rock. But even these plants vanish as your steps take you to the summit, where snow glistens all year long.

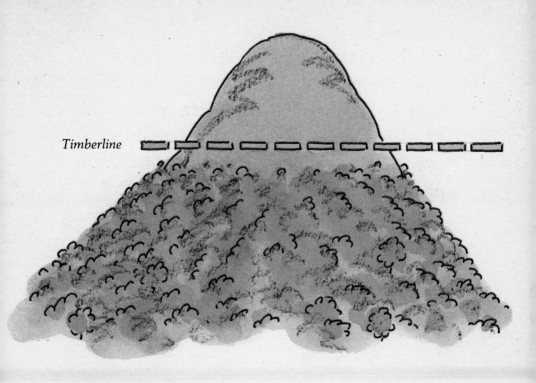

Timberline

The timberline, or tree line, is found at different heights in different parts of the world. Most trees will not grow above the timberline. On mountains close to the equator, the timberline is at a much higher altitude than on mountains in colder climates. In the coldest parts of the world, there are mountains without any plant life.

What is true for plant life on mountains is also true for animal life. As you go higher up a mountain, you will find fewer animals. The most common mountain creatures are small rodents, such as the mountain vole, pika, and rock marmot.

In the winter, bigger animals—such as

mountain goats and bighorn sheep—move down the mountain to find food. But the small rodents move into underground nests, where they live on the food they have stored during the warmer seasons. Some rodents, like the ground squirrel, hibernate until spring.

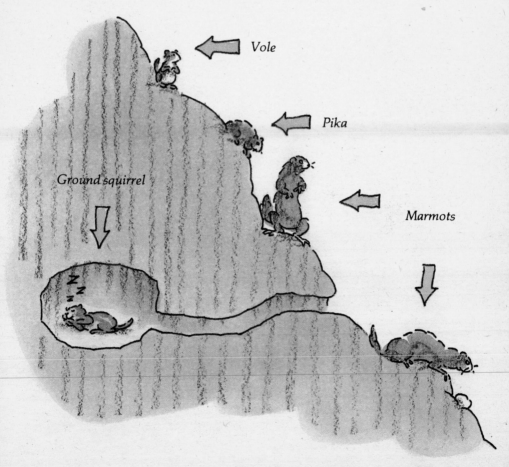

Vole

Pika

Ground squirrel

Marmots

Of all the mountain creatures, birds do best, especially the eagles, vultures, and hawks. These large birds are strong, swift flyers and have keen eyesight. These qualities enable them to hunt the small animals of the alpine meadows. But winter cold also drives most of the birds down to warm places.

All over the world people make their living from the mountains. Many South American lead and tin mines are located at high altitudes. And there are farms near the timberline in many countries.

Throughout the world people who live at high altitudes have certain things in common. Both the Indians in the South American mountains and the Asians in the Himalayan mountains of Tibet have larger lungs than people who live at sea level, so they can get more oxygen from the thin mountain air.

Throughout history, people have always been fascinated by mountains of all kinds. People come to the mountains to work, and they come to play. They come to climb the rocky slopes and to conquer the snow-capped peaks. They come to breathe the fresh mountain air and to relax by the icy glacial lakes. And they come to gaze in wonder at the soaring peaks that are wreathed in clouds.

It doesn't matter what kinds of mountains they are—dome, folded, fault block, or volcanic—all mountains are truly marvelous works of nature in our ever-changing world.